ARNOLDS AUZIŅŠ
ICE CREAM

TRANSLATED BY
ULDIS BALODIS AND KATE WAKELING

ILLUSTRATED BY LĪVA PITERĀNE

A modern nursery rhyme
from Latvia #005

MUM'S ALL HOT AND BOTHERED THAT

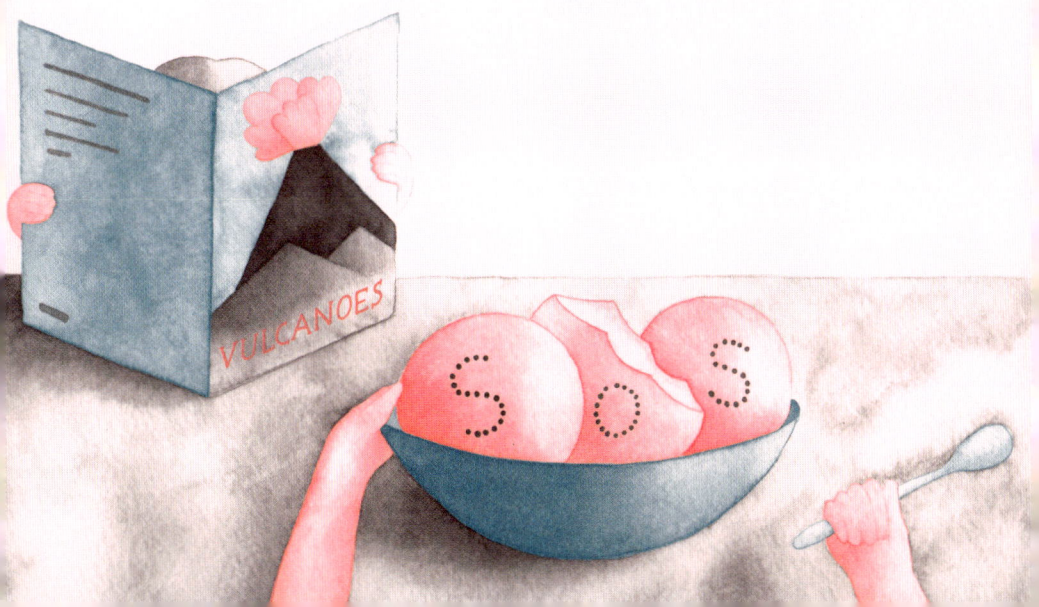

HOW HE WORSHIPS ICE CREAM,

WITH NO RULES REQUIRED, NO BAN.

THAT'S RIGHT, HE'S NOW A....
SNOWMAN.

Supported by Latvian Writers' Union (*Latvijas Rakstnieku Savienība*)
and Ministry of Culture of the Republic of Latvia

First published in the UK in 2018 by the Emma Press, Birmingham
Originally published in 2015 as "Saldējums" by Liels un mazs, Riga, Latvia

Text © Arnolds Auziņš, 1973
English-language translation © Uldis Balodis and Kate Wakeling, 2018
Illustrations © Līva Piterāne, 2015

BICKI-BOOKS
Artistic director – Rūta Briede
Design – Rūta Briede and Artis Briedis

Printed in Latvia by *Talsu tipogrāfijā*
on *Scandia 2000 Natural* 150 gsm and *Scandia 2000 Natural* 300 gsm

A CIP catalogue record of this book is available from the British Library
All rights reserved.

ISBN 978-1-910139-97-4
theemmapress.com